PAUL ROBESON

Scott Ehrlich

MELROSE SQUARE PUBLISHING COMPANY
LOS ANGELES, CALIFORNIA

Senior Consulting Editor for Chelsea House
Nathan Irvin Huggins
Director
W.E.B. Du Bois Institute for Afro-American Research
Harvard University

Consulting Editors for Melrose Square
Raymond Friday Locke
Antony Stately

Cover Painting: Jesse   Santos
Cover Design: Jeff Renfro   ISBN 0-87067-552-4

PAUL
ROBESON

CONTENTS

CONTENTS

Freedom
of
Speech

Chapter One

Freedom of Speech

O N THE MORNING of June 12, 1956, a panel of grim-faced government officials in Washington, D.C., assembled to review information about a hearing that was about to begin. Members of the House Un-American Activities Committee (HUAC), the officials were part of an investigative body that had been established by Congress in 1939 to look into the affairs of American citizens who were suspected by the government of acting against the interests of their country. Among those called before the committee to testify about their political beliefs were many prominent

While becoming an internationally famous singer and actor, Robeson aroused a great amount of controversy as an advocate of civil rights and freedom of speech.

Robeson was extremely vocal in his denunciation of the House Un-American Activities Committee, which was established by Congress to investigate the spread of communism in the United States.

citizens who had done nothing wrong except to disagree with their government's policies. Some of these people had been sent to prison simply for refusing to disclose their political beliefs before the committee.

On this spring day, the HUAC panel was going to be questioning Paul Robeson, the renowned singer and actor. During his long career on the stages of Europe and the United States, the 58-year-old Robeson had become one of the world's best-known and most beloved black Americans especially abroad. Yet he had not been content to be only an entertainer. For more than 20 years, he had been using his unforgettable bass voice to speak out

Robeson's wife, Eslanda, shared in her husband's work and political activism. She is shown here testifying before a Senate subcommittee in 1953.

about the needs and aspirations of the poor and oppressed people in the United States and around the world.

However, Robeson's ardent support for human rights causes had gained him many enemies. His statements that racism was still rampant within the United States were viewed by some Americans as being unpatriotic. His concerts in support of international peace, workers' rights, and racial tolerance had been picketed by his opponents, and violence had broken out at some of the events. In 1950, the State Department had revoked his passport, and he had since been confined within the United States and subjected to many forms of harassment. He had been blacklisted in the entertainment industry. (His name had been placed on a list of people who should not be hired because of their unpopular political beliefs.) Concert halls, stages, and recording and film studios were closed to him. Although he had continued to speak and sing wherever he could, by the time of his meeting with the HUAC, Robeson's spectacular voice had been virtually silenced because he was believed to be dangerous.

The removal of Robeson from the public stage was a tragedy for the United States. The country needed courageous people who were willing to speak out for international

Members of an anticommunist organization take down the license plate numbers of cars parked outside a Robeson concert in Oakland, California. In the 1950s, it was politically dangerous to be associated with an accused communist such as Robeson.

understanding and to propose solutions to America's racial problems. However, since the establishment of the HUAC, the United States had been caught up in a public hunt for traitors, subversives, spies, and members of left-wing organizations such as the Communist party.

During the late 1940s and early 1950s, Senator Joseph McCarthy had been the leader of the crusade to rid the government and American society of the so-called Red Menace, the alleged plot by communist agents to destroy the country. By the time Robeson was called before the HUAC, McCarthy was no longer in power. Yet the campaign against suspected communist sympathizers such as Robeson continued.

It seemed that many Americans wanted to hear Robeson answer only one question: Was he a member of the Communist party? Again and again, he answered the question: No, he was not a party member.

Robeson eventually decided that he would no longer answer this question. By giving any response, he felt that he would be violating the principle of free speech and admitting that holding communist views was illegal. Although he had never belonged to the American Communist party, he sympathized with the communist system in which there is public ownership of all goods. He had stood up for the rights of workers and for labor causes that were unpopular with supporters of America's capitalist system. Robeson and many of his friends were being persecuted for their political beliefs, and he felt that this persecution was clearly illegal according to the U.S. Constitution.

Robeson was a victim of the tensions arising from the global power struggle between the United States and the Soviet Union. These two nations had been allies during World War II, joining forces with other countries to crush Nazi Germany in 1945. Robeson was greatly admired in the Soviet Union and gave concerts there in the 1930s. During World War II, he helped to marshal American aid for the hard-pressed Soviet troops that were trying to turn back the Nazi invasion of the Soviet Union.

After the war ended, the Americans and the Soviets unleashed propaganda attacks against each other in their fight to control strategic global areas. The United States was determined to foster the growth of capitalist economies in other nations; the Soviets were equally committed to foster communist state-run economies. The two countries also began to stockpile powerful arsenals of nuclear weapons, and the terrifying possibility of total destruction of the human race added greatly to the fear and distrust felt between the Americans and the Soviets. Robeson felt that people should speak out against this increase in tension, yet his own voice was not allowed to be heard.

On the day of his hearing before the HUAC, Robeson was determined that his voice would be heard again. Few people had been strong enough to stand up for themselves in the face of the intense public pressure placed upon them by the HUAC and the anticommunist crusaders. But Robeson, who stood 6 feet 3

The originators of the "Red Menace" hysteria—(from left to right) Roy Cohn, Senator Joseph McCarthy, and Francis Carr—listen to testimony being given during a HUAC hearing.

inches tall and weighed more than 200 pounds, was more than able to take care of himself. He had recently fought a hard battle against the government to regain his legal rights to travel abroad.

Robeson had been told by government officials and spokesmen for the entertainment industry that the blacklisting against him would end if he stopped speaking out on controversial subjects. Yet he had not backed down. As he sat before the HUAC, he knew that his ability to make a living in his chosen profession in the United States might well depend on what happened at the hearing. The chairman of the HUAC was Representative Francis Walter, who had cosponsored the McCarran-Walter Act that allowed the attorney general of the United States to deport from the country any immigrants who were suspected of being sympathetic to communism. Walter and his associates on the committee were determined to show that Robeson was deeply involved in a dangerous network of communist organizers.

The meeting opened with a speech by Walter describing how Americans involved in the "communist conspiracy" against their own country were using their passports to travel abroad and, by some unspecified means, assist the forces seeking to undermine the U.S.

government. Although Robeson's lawyer asked that his client not be questioned about his passport troubles because his case was being reviewed in federal court and could be jeopardized by the hearing's discussions, the request was denied. The committee asked Robeson why he would not agree to the State Department's demand that he sign a statement that he was not a communist an action that would have allowed him to regain his passport. Declaring that such a requirement was unconstitutional, Robeson promised that the Supreme Court would eventually decide that the travel restrictions imposed on him were illegal.

The HUAC then asked the question: Was Robeson a member of the Communist party? Robeson bridled, demanding to know why the communists had less right than the Democrats or Republicans to form a political party. He also asked if his questioner wanted to follow him into the voting booth on election day. Robeson was instructed to give a direct answer to the question. He then invoked the fifth amendment, the constitutional law that gives all citizens appearing in judicial proceedings the right to refuse to answer a question if the answer might incriminate them.

As the hearing proceeded, Robeson responded to the committee's questions in different

Attending a civil rights congress, Robeson adds his name to a petition seeking to abolish the House Un-American Activities Committee.

ways. Asked again whether he was a communist, Robeson praised the bravery of the Russian armies in the recent war against the Nazis. Asked if he was listed under a pseudonym on the membership rolls of the Communist party, Robeson laughed and said the question was ludicrous. Asked if he knew various people whom the committee suspected of being communists, he invoked the fifth amendment after the mention of each name.

Robeson's spirited defense blunted the efforts to trap him. A lawyer himself, he questioned the committee as to whether their hearings were legal. He then attacked the McCarran-Walter Act, saying that it was keeping "all kinds of decent people" out of the country. Walter told Robeson that the law would exclude "only your kind" from America. Robeson responded that by saying "your kind," the congressman meant "black people."

The confrontational hearing continued. Robeson asked to be allowed to read a prepared statement that contained a strong attack on the HUAC, an eloquent appeal for the end to the oppression of blacks and workers, and a list of organizations from around the world that had invited him to speak. When he was told that he could read the statement only if he named the alleged communists who had helped him write it, Robeson exploded. He said that he had agreed to appear at the hearing only because he wanted to discuss the injustices faced by black Americans and oppressed workers.

"I am being tried for fighting for the rights of my people," Robeson said, claiming that nowhere in the United States were blacks treated as full citizens. "That is why I am here," he continued. "You want to shut up every

Encountering protests over his politics, Robeson maintained, "I shall take my voice wherever there are those who want to hear the melody of freedom or the words that might inspire hope and courage in the face of despair and fear."

Negro who has the courage to stand up and fight for the rights of his people, for the rights of workers."

Unmoved by Robeson's remarks, the committee members cited some black Americans who had spoken out against him. He countered by listing awards that he had received from numerous respected black organizations. When he was questioned about his visits to the Soviet Union and why, if he liked that country so much, he had not stayed there, Robeson responded, "Because my father was a slave, and my people died to build this country, and I am going to stay here and have a part of it, just like you."

After several more angry exchanges, during which Robeson's allegiance to the United States was attacked, he told the committee members, "You are the nonpatriots, and you are the un-Americans and you ought to be ashamed of yourselves." Finally, upset by the way Robeson was badgering the committee, Walter declared that the meeting was adjourned. Outside the building, Robeson discussed the hearing with members of the press.

By any measure, Robeson's appearance in front of the HUAC was extraordinary and was

During the HUAC hearings, many Americans—including the ones inside the van shown here—were sent to prison simply because their political views differed from those of the U.S. government.

one of the most intelligent and courageous performances of his life. The committee had not been able to prove that Robeson was a communist or that he had participated in any conspiracies against the U.S. government. Instead, the hearing had shown that Robeson was a man who would not desert his cause, no matter how intense the pressure. He was still blacklisted and his right to travel abroad had not yet been restored, but for at least one day his voice had been heard loudly and clearly across America.

Stages
of
Development

Chapter Two

Stages
of
Development

PAUL LEROY ROBESON was born on April 9, 1898, in Princeton, New Jersey. The youngest of five children, he was part of a large, supportive family that included many of his father's relatives. From an early age, he possessed a strong sense of family history and of the role that certain great events had played in shaping the place of blacks in American society.

Paul's mother, Maria Louisa Bustill, had mixed African, Cherokee Indian, and white ancestry. Her great-great-grandfather Cyrus Bustill had baked bread for George Washington's

In the New Jersey towns where Robeson was raised, the church played a central role in black community life.

starving troops at Valley Forge during the American Revolution and had also helped to found the Free African Society, America's first black mutual-aid organization. Many of the Bustills were artists, teachers, and scholars. They were also Quakers, who believed in pacifism and were strongly opposed to slavery. In the era before the Civil War, the Bustills helped run the underground railroad, a network of shelters established by antislavery activists to

TLE OF
KEN'S BEND

Robeson's father was among the many blacks who enlisted in the Union army during the Civil War to fight against slavery. This woodcut depicts a black regiment fighting at the Battle of Milliken's Bend.

aid runaway slaves as they attempted to escape to safe areas in the North and Canada.

The Reverend William Drew Robeson, Paul's father, was born a slave on a plantation near Raleigh, North Carolina, in 1845. At the age of 15, he escaped to the North by way of the underground railroad. When the Civil War broke out, William Robeson enlisted in the Union army and joined the fight to end slavery. After the war ended, he worked to gain an education. He eventually enrolled at Lincoln University, a black school near Philadelphia, Pennsylvania, where he studied to become a minister. After his graduation, he received a position at a church in Wilkes-Barre, Pennsylvania.

While William Robeson was attending college, he met Maria Bustill, who was then a schoolteacher in Philadelphia. The two were married in 1878 and moved to Princeton, New Jersey, a short time later, when William Robeson was appointed minister of the Witherspoon Street Presbyterian Church and its black congregation. Princeton was a long-established, prosperous, and conservative community, where many of the blacks in the town worked as servants in the households of the

Woodrow Wilson, who would become the 28th president of the United States, served as president of Princeton University at a time when the Robesons were living nearby.

officials and professors of Princeton University. Among these blacks were Reverend Robeson's relatives, who had left their homes in North Carolina to join him in the North, where there were supposedly more opportunities for blacks.

Maria Robeson helped her husband compose his sermons, assisted in his community work, and raised their five children: Bill, Ben, Reeve, Marion, and Paul. While she performed these duties, her eyesight was gradually being destroyed by cataracts. In 1904, just before Paul's sixth birthday, his mother bumped against a stove, upset some hot coals onto her dress, and was burned to death. Shock obliterated all of Paul's memories of her except for what she looked like in her coffin. He knew her only in terms of what others reported of her powerful intellect and of the strength, character, and spirit with which she had aided his father's work.

The school system that Paul entered in Princeton was segregated, and education above the primary level was for whites only; Paul's brother Bill had to travel to Trenton, New Jersey, to attend high school. Blacks were not allowed to attend Princeton University, either except for a few students who were studying to become ministers at the theological school. Although Reverend Robeson knew

ANNOTATIONS for PROGRAM

Obstinacy .... Bianchini

Say, shall I love you
Yes, I will love you!

Say, shall I suffer!
Yes, I will suffer!

Say, shall I die'
Yes, I will die!

Say, shall I go!
No . . . I shall stay!

Se Florindo e Fedele ... Alessandro Scarlatti

Should Florindo be faithful
Surely I'll fail in love.
How artful e'er he draw the bow
Well vers'd in archers wiles.
My heart I can defend, I know.
From any luring smiles.
Sighing, weeping, and imploring
My breast can never move:
But if he should be faithful
I'll surely fall in love.

But my Bird is Long in Homing ... Sibelius

On the lake the swan is mirror'd,
Snowy-white the seabirds flutter:
High in heav'n the lark is singing,
Hark, the curlew o'er the moorland.

Spring has revis'd all her forces

NEGRO SPIRITUALS

"Deep River" .... (Arr. Burleigh)

Deep river, my home is over Jordan.
Deep river, Lord. I want to cross over
Into camp around to don't you want to 1.?

Is that gospel feast, that promised land
where all is peace?
O' Deep river, Lord, I want to cross
over into campground.

"Heav'n! Heav'n!" .... Laurence Brown

I got a robe, you got a robe,
All God's children got a robe.
When I get to Heav'n going to put on my robe.
Going to shout all over God's Heav'n
Heav'n! Heav'n!
Everybody talking about Heav'n
Aint going there.

I got shoes, you got shoes,
All God's children got shoes.
When I get to Heav'n going to put on my shoes,
Going to walk all over God's Heav'n.
Heav'n! Heav'n!
Everbody talking about Heav'n
Aint going there.

"Crucifixion" .... Payne

Lovingly the day doth lure them.

I alone am longing ever
Darkness and regret to scatter,
Longing in my heart to cherish,
Friendly warmth of spring and gladness,

Like a golden hour of sunshine
I am glad, despite my sorrow,
Smiling thru the tears that blind me,
But my bird is long in homing.

Idle Wishes ⸻ *Sibelius*

What numberless waves are wand'ring
Where ocean's path shimmers blue
O, would that I were among them,
A wave of the Ocean too.

Unmoved in the depths of my spirit
So careless chilly so clear
So free from desires and memories,
Of distant days that were dear.

But, were I a wandering billow,
Would life be so alter'd for me?
Here, too, with a flock I wander,
As cold as waves of the sea.

They trifle with joy and with sorrow,
With tears and laughter they play
My heart is alone in its fervour.
O, would I were heartless as they.

No a word.

They pierced him in the side —
An' he never said a mumb'lin word.
Not a word.

He bow'd his head an' died —
An' he never said a mumb'lin word.
Not a word, not a word, not a word.

"My Soul's Been Anchored in the Lord" *Price*

In the Lord, in the Lord.
My soul's been anchored in the Lord.

Before I'd stay in Hell one day,
My soul's been anchored in the Lord.
I'd sing and pray myself away,
My soul's been anchored in the Lord.

I'm going to pray and never stop.
My soul's been anchored in the Lord.
Until I reach the mountain top.
My soul's been anchored in the Lord.

In the Lord, in the Lord.
My soul's been anchored in the Lord.
God knows my soul's been anchored in the Lord.

(Continued)

*Throughout his life, Robeson sought to popularize Negro spirituals,
which were derived from slaves' work songs. He first heard these
spirituals in his father's church.*

the university's president, Woodrow Wilson (who would later become president of the United States), no exceptions to enrollment policies were made not even for promising black students such as Bill Robeson.

Despite the color line in Princeton, the Reverend Robeson was well respected in the town by both blacks and whites, who realized the central role that the church played in black community life. The church was Paul's second home. Loved by his father, brothers, sister, and the closely knit black community, he rarely felt like a motherless child while he was growing up.

In church, Paul learned Negro spirituals and other songs of his people and listened to the

Educator Booker T. Washington believed that the best way for blacks to improve their social standing was by performing necessary services for whites.

deep-voiced "singing" sermons that his father gave from the pulpit. At home, Paul and his brothers often gathered around their father and sang harmony songs while the reverend played the piano. When people later commented on Paul's incredibly powerful voice, he would say that they should have heard his father—*he* had a voice.

Paul's Princeton days were relatively happy ones. He loved to play football in vacant lots with his brothers, and he also enjoyed playing checkers with his father, whom he adored. Although he did not attend an integrated school, he experienced less prejudice while he was growing up than did black children who were raised in the South, where Jim Crow laws enforced segregation. Discrimination certainly existed in Princeton. However, Paul, who knew little about his father's slave upbringing because the Reverend Robeson never spoke about his life as a slave, escaped the effects of extreme racial bigotry.

Paul's brother Bill was the best student in the family, and he helped inspire Paul's deep love of learning. Their brother Ben encouraged Paul's interest in sports. Their sister, Marion, who later became a schoolteacher like their mother, filled Paul with warmth and good humor. And their brother Reeve taught Paul to stand up for himself. Reeve often got into trouble with the law in Princeton by striking back when insulted by bigoted university students. He carried a bag of jagged rocks for self-defense, and he emptied it so often that the Reverend Robeson eventually had to ask Reeve to leave town to spare young Paul his dangerous example.

However, it was Reverend Robeson who had the strongest influence on Paul's life. The reverend's unbending belief in the importance of personal integrity and achievement shaped Paul's character. He was taught not to be satisfied with anything less than his best effort, and his report cards reflected his determination to succeed. Reverend Robeson disagreed with the belief made popular by the noted black educator Booker T. Washington that the education of blacks should be limited to only those subjects that would help them prepare for the workplace. The reverend insisted that Latin, Greek, history, philosophy, and literature should be part of any education. Strongly committed to racial equality, the reverend stated that an individual's success held no meaning unless it also benefited his or her people. Accordingly, he encouraged Paul to learn about the history of black Americans and of the ancient civilizations of Africa.

In 1906, Reverend Robeson lost his position at his church after a dispute with members of the congregation. Without complaint, he bought a horse and wagon, and he earned money by hauling ashes and ferrying Princeton University students around town. A year later, he changed his religious denomination, moved the family to Westfield, New Jersey, and built the Downing Street African Methodist Episcopal Zion Church.

Westfield was not as wealthy or as strictly segregated as Princeton. The few black students in town were free to go to the same public schools attended by white children. In Westfield's working-class neighborhoods, Paul often visited white homes, never realizing his easy movement between the black and white communities was unusual. His father's strong reputation helped him win acceptance, but his own abilities at sports and schoolwork and his eager friendliness were even more instrumental in opening doors.

In 1910, when Paul was 12 years old, his father became pastor of the St. Thomas African Methodist Episcopal Zion Church in Somerville, New Jersey. The family moved once again. In eighth grade at the time, Paul attended a respected all-black school in the area and graduated at the top of his class. The following year, he became one of two black students enrolled at Somerville High School. An excellent student, the tall, strong young man made a tremendous impression as an athlete, playing fullback on the high school football team. He formed close friendships with white classmates and received strong

In trying out for the Rutgers football team, Robeson displayed his characteristic resolve: He overcame the team's racial prejudices and soon became a star running back.

encouragement from his teachers. The music instructor took a special interest in training Paul's voice, and his English teacher gave him his first opportunity on the stage, choosing him for the title role in the school production of William Shakespeare's play *Othello*.

Although Paul was developing a powerful public-speaking style through his activity in the school's debating club, he did not feel ready to act in one of Shakespeare's plays. However, he prepared intensively for the role, studying photographs of actors who had played the part of the tormented Moorish general Othello. Every photograph showed Othello as having a beard. This detail obsessed Paul, and just before the play's first performance he found what he needed: a long white beard from a Santa Claus costume. The audience was shocked when he appeared on stage with the strange-looking beard glued to his face. When Paul tried to recite his lines, he discovered that he could not be heard clearly through the beard's thick white strands. In desperation, he turned his back to the audience and tore off the beard, taking bits of skin with it. He then continued his performance, ignoring the pain that was the result of his having torn off some of his skin. It was such a horrible experience that no one could have convinced him he would ever try acting again.

One person marred Paul's happiness at Somerville High School: the principal, Dr. Ackerman, who could not conceal his racism. The better Paul's performance in school, the greater Ackerman's hostility. Because Paul was a model student, Ackerman had few opportunities to criticize him. He tried unsuccessfully to convince the music teacher not to choose Paul as the glee club's soloist and was reduced to making petty notes about the few times when Paul was late to class.

Ackerman finally got his chance to snub Paul when Rutgers University in nearby New Brunswick, New Jersey, established a statewide competition for full four-year scholarships. He simply neglected to inform the school's prize student about the scholarship. By the time Paul found out about the scholarship, he had already missed the preliminary examination, which was based on the subjects covered in the first three years of high school. To qualify for the scholarship, Paul had to take a test dealing with all of the courses he had studied in high school. The other students were only being examined on their final year's studies.

With the encouragement of friends and teachers and with the ill will of Ackerman goading him on, Paul studied furiously and won the scholarship. He felt that he would be happier at Lincoln University, his father's alma mater, than at Rutgers, but he was too proud of winning the scholarship to consider giving it up. His victory had proved to him that he could overcome unequal and unfair circumstances. The local black community was also aware of Paul's unlimited potential. He later wrote: "Like my father, the people claimed to see something special about me. Whatever it was, and no one really said, they felt I was fated for great things to come."

In the spring of 1915, Paul entered a statewide public-speaking contest, reciting the 19th-century antislavery leader Wendell Phillips's essay on Toussaint L'Ouverture, the former slave who led a successful rebellion of the black inhabitants of the Caribbean nation of Haiti against French rule. The idea for this reading came from Paul's brother Bill, who had become a medical doctor in Washington, D.C. Paul was not troubled that he was reading a searing attack on the concept of white supremacy to an almost all-white audience. He had no notion then, as he would later on, of challenging the established order. He merely concentrated on his diction so that the contest's judges would rate him highly. He finished in third place.

Just as 17-year-old Paul was entering Rutgers University in 1915, Booker T. Washington, the American black community's

longtime leading spokesman, was near death.
Many of Washington's beliefs about the prop-
er place of blacks in the United States were
coming under attack by a younger generation
of leaders who thought that Washington was
too accepting of segregationist laws and was
not fighting hard enough for black equality.
The recently formed National Association for

The star catcher on the Rutgers varsity baseball team, Robeson (front row, second from right) won 15 sports letters while he was in college.

the Advancement of Colored People (NAACP) was pressing the campaign for greater black political, educational, and occupational opportunities. A strong believer in academics, Paul was at the forefront of this new movement for higher learning for blacks.

As an incoming freshman at Rutgers University, Paul wanted to continue his studies of

Latin, Greek, physics, math, and history, and he wanted to play football. Rutgers had a highly successful football team, and the coach, Foster Sanford, wanted the massively built freshman on the squad. But all of the team's varsity members were white, and many of them were opposed to playing alongside a black man. Paul tried out for the team, but on the first day of practice a player punched him in the face and broke his nose. Paul fell flat on his back. Then another player fell on him, dislocating Paul's shoulder.

Paul's immediate reaction was that he should give up and go home, but his father had impressed on him that he was the representative of his race, the embodiment of all black Americans who wanted to play football, go to college, and live as freely as any other citizen. The Reverend Robeson had taught his son that he must stand up for his rights and refuse to accept any action that violated his sense of human dignity.

Paul spent 10 days in bed recovering from his injuries before returning to the football field. After he made his first tackle, a player stepped on his hand. The cleats of the football shoe tore off the fingernails.

For the first time in Paul's life, he became consumed with rage. On the next play, the ball carrier and a group of blockers ran at him.

Knocking down the three blockers, he grabbed the ball carrier and lifted him over his head. Just as he was about to throw the player to the ground, Coach Sanford stopped him by shouting, "Robey, you're on the varsity."

Robeson quickly became a star football player, and his teammates, who had done so much to hurt him, soon became his friends. Characteristically, his athletic career did not interfere with his studies. In 1918, he was elected to a select national honors society, Phi Beta Kappa. By his senior year he had won 15 sports

Robeson was still in college when he began to speak out about the need for racial understanding and educational opportunities for blacks.

letters, not only in football but in basketball, baseball, and track and field. He was twice elected to the collegiate All-American football team, and he also won a prize for public speak-

ing. His senior thesis, entitled "The Fourteenth Amendment, the Sleeping Giant of the American Constitution," was a scholarly yet passionate examination of the constitutional

Robeson (at left) with fellow members of the Cap and Skull, an honors society at Rutgers. Always an excellent student, he graduated first in his class from the university.

amendment that guarantees all U.S. citizens their civil rights and forbids any state to pass laws that infringe upon these rights. In many parts of the country, the law was being violated and blacks were being denied the opportunity to vote or attend the schools of their choice. Robeson was growing strongly committed to helping lead the battle for these rights.

The valedictorian of his class, Robeson delivered the commencement speech at his graduation ceremonies in 1919. In his address, entitled "The New Idealism," he said:

> We of the younger generation especially must feel a sacred call to that which lies before us. I go out to do my little part in helping my untutored brother. We of this less-favored race realize that our future lies chiefly in our own hands...And we are struggling on, attempting to show that knowledge can be obtained under difficulties... neither the old-time slavery, nor continued prejudice need extinguish self-respect, crush manly ambition, or paralyze effort.

It was a speech that would have pleased Reverend Robeson, who had died during his son's junior year at Rutgers. The reverend had hoped that his youngest son would follow him into the ministry, but Robeson did not heed the call. He wanted desperately to fulfill his father's dream of serving his people even though he had no idea how to achieve this goal. Coach Sanford then suggested that he become a lawyer and battle for the rights of his people in court. Robeson readily agreed. He enrolled in the law school at Columbia University and moved to New York City.

In announcing Robeson's graduation, one newspaper called the distinguished student "one of the biggest all-around college men and athletes that this country has ever known."

A
Rising
Star

Chapter Three

A
Rising
Star

WHEN ROBESON arrived in New York City in the middle of 1919, he decided to settle in Harlem, an area that was rapidly becoming the leading center of black American culture and political activity. The surge in black artistic achievement, which would become known as the Harlem Renaissance, was attracting writers such as Langston Hughes, Countee Cullen, and Jean Toomer to the area. Jazz had arrived from the Deep South and was about to become the favorite music of many Americans. White audiences were flocking to the Lafayette Theatre and

Robeson's career as a professional singer began in 1925 with a recital of black spirituals at the Greenwich Village Theater in New York.

other popular Harlem night spots for music, dance, and theater shows.

The rapid growth of the black population in Harlem during the early 1900s had been mirrored in many other cities in the North. From 1915 to 1918, while World War I was being fought in Europe, thousands of blacks left farms in the South and moved to the North to take better-paying jobs in the factories that produced weapons and other supplies. However, when the war ended in 1918 and industrial production slowed down, the white

Black nationalist leader Marcus Garvey labored to achieve racial pride and economic self-sufficiency for blacks by calling for black Americans to leave the United States and move to Africa.

populations in northern cities began to feel threatened by the black migration. Racial tensions exploded into riots in many cities during the summer of 1919. Led by Marcus Garvey, the black nationalist organization known as the Universal Negro Improvement Association had formed its own steamship company and was trying to interest blacks in moving back to Africa.

In the protective environment of Harlem, the 21-year-old Robeson was shielded from much of the racial animosity that was so

Prominent scholar W. E. B. Du Bois believed in agitating for social and political change at a time when other black leaders were advocating vocational training as the key to black advancement.

evident elsewhere in the country. At that time, the jazz musicians Noble Sissle and Eubie Blake were preparing to present *Shuffle Along*, an all-black musical, on Broadway. Sissle and Blake were having lunch in a restaurant one afternoon when Robeson stopped by for an ice cream. The two composers instantly recognized the famous Rutgers football star. They did not know whether Robeson could sing, but one look at his intense, imposing figure convinced them he belonged on the stage. However, he became involved in coaching a football team for the summer before they could arrange an audition for him.

Robeson worked at a variety of jobs to pay his way through law school. He had worked ever since he was 14 years old, when his brother Ben had found him a job in the kitchen of a seaside hotel in Narragansett, Rhode Island. Ben waited on tables in the hotel whereas his younger brother cleaned pots and pans, peeled potatoes, and mopped the floors from early in the morning until late in the evening. It was miserable work, but Robeson made many friends there, so he returned to the job during most of the summers of his college years. After his father died, he had to work even more to support himself.

Immediately upon entering Columbia Law

School, Robeson became consumed in his work and studies. He had little time to enjoy Harlem's cultural life, although he was pleased to have the chance to speak with the prominent black intellectual and writer W. E. B. Du Bois at a party on New Year's Eve. The leader of the NAACP and editor of the organization's newspaper, the *Crisis*, Du Bois was seeking to arouse black resistance to segregationist laws and racial violence. Robeson was strongly influenced by Du Bois's movement for black equality.

With the help of Foster Sanford, Robeson landed a part-time position in a law firm. He wrote legal briefs (preparatory arguments) for cases that were to be heard in court. He also sought to earn money by acting. He played the lead role in the Harlem YWCA's 1920 production of *Simon the Cyrenian*. This one-act play, which deals with the black man who was supposed to have carried Christ's cross, was directed by Charles Gilpin, then one of the best-known black actors in America. Gilpin had previously appeared on Broadway in Eugene O'Neill's epic drama *The Emperor Jones*.

On the night of the first performance of *Simon the Cyrenian*, Robeson was delayed at his law office and arrived late for the show. Before he stepped onto the stage, he could not remember his lines even though he had tried to study on the subway on his way to the theater. Also, he was nervous because he had lost an important page from the script. But just before the play began, he saw himself as the Harlem audience perceived him, as he had perceived himself on another different stage, the football field: He was a star. This sense of confidence enabled Robeson to give a stellar performance. After the show, he was warmly congratulated by members of the Provincetown Players, an actors' group that was also based in New York, in a theater in Greenwich Village. The group featured works by Eugene O'Neill, the young playwright whose dark emotional dramas were beginning to receive much critical notice.

The early 1920s were a good time for a black actor like Robeson to be making his mark on the stage. Before starring in *Simon the Cyrenian*, he had worked briefly as an understudy in Sissle and Blake's *Shuffle Along*. The success of this musical, along with the shows at the Lafayette Theatre, was creating a great deal of excitement. *The Chocolate Dandies*, a show that featured a sensational new dancer named Josephine Baker, was also helping to

Dancer Josephine Baker was one of the many black artists and performers responsible for popularizing black culture in the 1920s, a period that came to be known as the Harlem Renaissance.

bring flocks of talent scouts to Harlem. Many black actors and dancers were being signed up for parts in Broadway productions and Hollywood films. Although the parts were often small, some of the new shows were beginning to feature blacks in serious roles—a welcome departure from the clownish depictions of blacks in earlier entertainments.

Along with acting on the stage, Robeson was also performing on the football field. During weekends in the fall of 1920, he played for a professional football team. Accordingly, he managed to support himself through a wide range of activities.

One of Robeson's few releases from the pressures of law school was basketball. In January 1921, he slipped on a gym floor, sprained his shoulder, and had to go to the Columbia Presbyterian Medical Center to have his arm put in a sling. While there, he met a pretty and extremely bright hospital technician named Eslanda Cardozo Goode. They had seen each other once before, in a coffee shop, but Robeson, uncharacteristically, had been drunk. Goode had subsequently thought that Robeson was a playboy. However, their second meeting was much friendlier. They soon became intimate friends, and by August 1921 they were married.

Like her husband, Eslanda Goode came from

While Robeson was determined to make a career for himself as a lawyer, he nevertheless chose to appear in the play Taboo *in 1922. He returned to law school once the show ended its tour of England.*

Robeson (third row from top, fifth from left) with the Columbia Law School graduating class in 1923. "At this time," he said, "I was an aspiring lawyer, believing that to succeed would help raise my peo-

ple, the Black people of the world. Theater and concerts were fur-thest from my mind."

a distinguished family. Her grandfather Francis Cardozo was born a slave in South Carolina but had been sent by his liberal-minded masters to be educated at the University of Glasgow in Scotland. He was active in the American antislavery movement before the Civil War. He later held high positions in the South Carolina state government and taught Latin at Howard University in Washington, D.C.

Born in 1896, Eslanda grew up in New York City. Her father died when she was young, and her mother worked as a masseuse so that Eslanda could go to college. After graduating with a degree in medical chemistry, Eslanda became one of the first blacks to work as an analytical chemist in a major hospital.

After Eslanda's marriage to Robeson, she continued to work while he finished up his law studies. He also continued to play professional football on weekends. In 1922, he appeared in the National Football League's championship game, playing for the Akron Indians against the Chicago Bears.

An excellent football player, Robeson impressed many people with his powerful physique. He was offered a great deal of money to fight Jack Dempsey, the reigning heavyweight champion, but he turned down the offer. He doubted that his father would have approved of his son becoming a prizefighter.

Having so many different careers going at once, Robeson was not sure whether he wanted to continue to pursue a career in acting or just concentrate on law. However, he made his choice in 1922, when the promise of a weekly salary lured him into a play called *Taboo*. When the play, renamed *Voodoo*, was booked for a tour through England in the summer, he received his first opportunity to travel abroad. He performed with the revered actress and director Mrs. Patrick Campbell, who was so impressed by Robeson's voice that she created opportunities for him to sing Negro spirituals in some of *Voodoo*'s scenes. During the tour, Robeson encountered so little prejudice toward blacks in England that he began to grow especially dissatisfied with the racial climate in his own country.

Upon returning to the United States, Robeson completed his studies at Columbia and graduated with a law degree in 1923. Among his hopes was that someday he would be able to stand before the highest courts in the land and represent poor and needy citizens. He wanted to help create laws that would protect all Americans from economic exploitation and racial injustices.

Following his graduation from Columbia, Robeson obtained a position in a prominent law firm. On occasion, he also sang at Harlem's

Playwright Eugene O'Neill (left) and musician Lawrence Brown (second from right) helped to launch Robeson in his artistic career. O'Neill's dark dramas and Brown's stirring arrangements of black spirituals provided him with showcases for his talents.

famed Cotton Club, where such famous entertainers as Florence Mills and Earl "Snakehips" Tucker performed. A racial incident ultimately prompted him to leave the legal profession. A white secretary with whom he was working refused to take dictation from him. An-

gered by her racism, Robeson quit the job.

The disappointment that Robeson felt when he left his job was lessened when Eugene O'Neill asked him to play the lead in the playwright's new drama, *All God's Chillun Got Wings*. In this production by the Provincetown

Players, Robeson would portray Jim Harris, a young law student whose soul is destroyed when his wife becomes insanely jealous about her husband's budding career. Jim is ultimately forced to give up his future, resigning himself to caring for his deranged wife. What raised the play above most domestic drama of the

time is the fact that Jim is black and his wife is white. Much of the play was considered distasteful by white audiences, who were especially offended by the final scene, in which Jim's wife kneels before him and kisses his hand.

Instead of introducing Robeson in such an

Robeson with costar Mary Blair in a performance of All God's Chillun Got Wings. *The play's portrayal of a racially mixed marriage caused a furor in both the black and white communities.*

incendiary role, James Light, the director of the Provincetown Players, decided that Robeson should first play the lead role in *The Emperor Jones*, stepping into the part that Charles Gilpin had made famous. The revival of the play opened on May 5, 1924, before a packed house waiting to see the handsome football star. Many of the critics attending the premiere were skeptical that he was skilled at doing anything more than blocking and tackling, but Robeson's interpretation of his role was a tremendous success. In the play, he portrayed Brutus Jones, an ex-railway attendant who creates a corrupt empire on a Caribbean island, only to be deposed by his subjects and then driven mad by jungle spirits. The part of Jones offered Robeson the chance to play a character with a far more complex personality than the roles usually given to blacks.

The success of *The Emperor Jones* production put even greater pressure on the cast of *All God's Chillun Got Wings*. Before the play opened, groups hostile to public portrayals of a racially mixed marriage raised a storm of protest about the play, and threats on Robeson's life were made by the white supremacist

Robeson as the beleaguered ruler in The Emperor Jones. *He was hailed for the dignity and depth of character that he brought to the role.*

organization, the Ku Klux Klan. O'Neill condemned the protests, many of which were made in ignorance of the play's contents. W. E. B. Du Bois praised O'Neill for his honesty and bravery, stating that the work "must be done. No greater mine of dramatic material ever lay ready for the great artist's hands than the situation of men of Negro blood in modern America."

Although black performers such as these appeared at the Cotton Club, the famous Harlem nightspot admitted white audiences only.

Following the premiere of *All God's Chillun Got Wings* on May 15, 1924, Robeson was criticized in the black press for accepting the role of Jim Harris. These critics believed that it was degrading for an intelligent, cultured black man to be portrayed as the virtual slave of his depraved white wife. However, many of these critics failed to appreciate O'Neill's brave attempt to examine the theme of racial misunderstanding.

Robeson's performance in *All God's Chillun Got Wings* was generally well praised, but the controversial play had only a short run. Afterward, Robeson told O'Neill of his desire to act in roles that examined the special problems faced by blacks in America. The playwright advised him not to limit himself just to the roles normally reserved for black actors but to play all of the great dramatic roles. Rather than portray largely symbolic and thinly fleshed out figures, Robeson became determined to take on roles that would allow him the chance to present complex human characters. He also came to believe that black writers were too self-conscious. They were afraid to reveal the least noble aspects of their lives, which were often the most dramatic.

In June 1924, Robeson starred in a play called *Rosanne* in Philadelphia. His performance was followed by a comment from

George Jean Nathan, dean of American theater critics, who wrote that despite Robeson's lack of training, he was among the most eloquent, impressive, and convincing actors to be seen in years.

At the same time that Robeson was making a strong impression on the stage, he also appeared in his first film, *Body and Soul*, a movie produced by the independent black filmmaker Oscar Micheaux. Robeson played a Georgia preacher who tries to conceal his real identity. Produced in the era just prior to the advent of sound in motion pictures, *Body and Soul* was a silent movie with subtitles.

Six years would pass before Robeson made another film. Not only were few roles offered to blacks by Hollywood filmmakers, but a serious artist such as Robeson was unable to find many parts that accurately portrayed the lives of black people.

Along with his film career, Robeson's singing career was also being launched in the early 1920s. It had taken a while for the power of his voice to be recognized. His songs in *Voodoo* and his performances at the Cotton Club had gained him some attention, but it was not until the rehearsals began for *The Emperor Jones* that his singing ability was really noticed. One scene in the play called for him to exit whistling, but Robeson was unable to whistle. The director suggested that he hum or sing instead. When the Provincetown Players heard him sing, they realized he had one of the greatest bass voices of any man alive.

A short time later, Robeson became reacquainted with Lawrence Brown, a young black pianist whom Robeson had met in London in 1922. A classically trained musician, Brown was also an authority on black folk music. After talking with Brown about the simple, haunting songs that Robeson had heard performed in the black community when he was growing up—spirituals, "singing" sermons given by preachers such as his father, work songs, and blues songs—he decided that he wanted to help black folk music win a larger audience. He believed that this music was one of the greatest art forms to be developed in America.

Robeson and Brown began to arrange a medley of black folk songs for public performance. They made their debut at a party given by the writer Carl Van Vechten, who was a great admirer of black artists and writers. Among the guests at the affair were such noted artists and patrons of the arts as composer George Gershwin, philanthropist Otto Kahn, publisher Alfred Knopf, and authors James Weldon Johnson, Elinor Wylie, and

Theodore Dreiser. In other private gatherings during the following weeks, Robeson and Brown gave more performances.

A concert was finally arranged for Robeson and Brown at the Greenwich Village Theater. Performing before a packed house on April 19, 1925, the two men received demands for so many encores that they went through the complete repertoire of songs they had rehearsed together, including such classics as "Go Down, Moses" and "Joshua Fit de Battle of Jericho." The critics praised Robeson's magnificent voice and his wonderfully emotive performance, but

By the mid-1920s, Robeson's plans to uplift his race through his work as a lawyer had been cast aside. Instead, he was pursuing a career as an entertainer, seeking to accomplish the same goal in a more popular manner.

they also were enthusiastic about black folk music, which Robeson and Brown were presenting for the first time as a major art form. Noting the intense feeling and conviction in Robeson's singing, one reviewer wrote about the spirituals: "Sung by one man, they voiced the sorrows and hopes of a people."

Robeson's career on the stage, screen, and in concert halls was beginning to blossom. In mid-1925, he was chosen to play the lead in the London stage production of *The Emperor Jones*, which was to be directed by James Light, the Provincetown Players' director. A rising star in America, Robeson soon set out for Europe, ready to conquer another world.

A
World of
Music

Chapter Four

A World of Music

LONDON WAS wonderfully receptive to the 27-year-old Robeson when he returned there in 1925. His performance in *The Emperor Jones* was a tremendous success. The critics praised the richness of his voice, although they were less complimentary of the play itself. Still, Robeson believed that he helped the London audiences "see a modern Negro roll up the centuries and reveal primeval man." He said that when he played the part of Brutus Jones, "civilization falls away from me. My plight becomes real; the horrors, terrible facts. I feel the terror of the slave mart,

Robeson's appearance in the film version of The Emperor Jones *helped to increase his popularity as an actor.*

After performing in the London run of The Emperor Jones, *Robeson took time off from his acting career to vacation on the French Riviera.*

the degradation of man bought and sold into slavery."

Eslanda accompanied Robeson to England, and the two of them grew to love the people and the city of London during the months they

stayed there. Like her husband, she was troubled by racial intolerance, so she was glad to be living in a city that seemed to be so accepting of blacks.

When the London run of *The Emperor*

Although Robeson's performance in Black Boy *was widely praised, the rest of the Broadway production was not well received.*

Jones ended, the Robesons decided to visit the French Riviera on the Mediterranean Sea. One morning, Robeson was lying on the beach when he heard a fisherman singing as he pulled in his nets. Robeson used the little

French that he knew to ask the man if he could join him on his next fishing expedition. After being offered some money, the fisherman agreed to the request.

When the two men went fishing together, Robeson tried to explain to the fisherman the difficulties of his work as an actor and singer. Unable to express himself, he began to sing, and his voice was heard by all of the fishermen who were casting their nets nearby. Robeson was taken home by the fisherman to sing for his family. The entire fishing village was soon being entertained by the man with the incredible voice. To show his appreciation to his hosts, Robeson bought part of their day's catch and sponsored a huge feast on the beach.

The Robesons made trips to Monte Carlo, Nice, and other cities along the Mediterranean. During their travels, they met some of Robeson's classmates from Rutgers and Columbia, most of whom were artists and writers. Like the fishermen, they found the Riviera to be a pleasant place to work.

During this time, Robeson met Claude McKay, a West Indian-born poet and novelist who was one of the most influential writers of the Harlem Renaissance. McKay excitedly told Robeson that he had been to the Soviet Union and was quite impressed with the achievements of the new communist workers' state.

He also introduced Robeson to other blacks who had moved to France to escape from the racial inequality that they experienced in America. Because there was so little work for black actors in America, Robeson was considering staying away from the country as well. He was thinking of traveling throughout the world, giving concert tours of black folk music.

Yet Robeson returned to the United States after his stay in southern France. He joined Lawrence Brown in an enormously successful cross-country concert tour, with Eslanda traveling with them as tour manager. However,

Paul Robeson, Jr., with his mother, Eslanda.

the discrimination that Robeson experienced in America was extremely distressing to him. After spending a few months in European cities where racial prejudice was barely evident, he and Eslanda began to think more and more of moving to Europe.

After the end of the concert tour, Robeson starred on Broadway in the play *Black Boy*. He was impressive in the role of a worthless drifter who rises up to win the world heavyweight boxing title, only to lose it after slipping back to former habits. Although it was not a very successful play, *Black Boy* helped enhance Robeson's stature as an actor.

In 1927, Robeson and Brown continued with their concert tour of America, while Eslanda remained in Harlem. The two men again received high critical praise for their renditions of such songs as "Swing Low, Sweet Chariot." In October, they traveled to Paris to give a concert and then continued on to perform in England, Romania, Greece, and Yugolavia. While on tour, Robeson received the news that he had a son. Eslanda had given birth to Paul Robeson, Jr., (nicknamed Pauli) on November 2.

Robeson returned to the United States to see his new son, but a few months later, in 1928, he and Eslanda decided that they would move to England and leave Pauli in America

Written by Jerome Kern with Robeson in mind, the song "Ol' Man River" soon became synonymous with the performer's relentless fight for freedom and world peace.

for a few months with Eslanda's mother while they got settled in London. Robeson continued to study folk music, and he soon began to discover close connections between the songs of black Americans and the traditional tunes of the people of England, Ireland, and Wales. He was particularly happy to be living in London at a time when people in Europe were becoming acquainted with jazz, the literature

Days with Paul Robeson

of the Harlem Renaissance, and African sculpture.

While Robeson was in London, he starred in *Show Boat*, a musical about life on the Mississippi River. The producers of *Show Boat* had thought that the part of the lazy worker Joe would be too small for him. However, the role called for Robeson to sing "Ol' Man River," a song written by Jerome Kern, one of the most important composers for the theater. The musical was greeted by sensational reviews after it opened in London, and Robeson's singing was especially praised. One critic called Robeson the "promise of his race" and the "idol of his people."

The English were as impressed with Robeson as he was with them. During the premiere run of *Show Boat* in 1928, he became the toast of the town and was invited to numerous parties by the most prominent people in London's high society. He took over the Drury Lane theater, where the musical was being performed, to give spirituals concerts on Sunday nights. Commenting on his performance, a local newspaper wrote that Robeson was not only a supremely talented actor and singer but "a great man, who creates the soul of a people in bondage and shows you its true kinship with the fettered soul of man."

In 1929, Robeson decided to make a concert tour of Ireland and the European continent, performing in Dublin, Ireland; Paris, France; Dresden, Germany; Warsaw, Poland; Prague, Czechoslovakia, and many other large cities. Once again, he was gratified that black folk music was so warmly received by the European audiences. However, when he returned to London after the tour, he experienced a bitter reminder of racial prejudice. Invited to a

Robeson appeared in many different productions of Othello throughout his career. This 1943 Broadway offering paired him with actress Uta Hagen, who played the ill-fated Desdemona.

party given by a friend in a London hotel, he was barred from entering the building because he was black. The incident was considered a great scandal by the British public, and the hotel management soon apologized to Robeson. Eventually, all of London's hotels promised to accept blacks as guests.

In November 1929, Robeson returned to the United States and sang before a sold-out house at New York's Carnegie Hall, adding songs from other countries to his repertoire of black American folk music. Among the additions were one song by Ludwig van Beethoven and two by Wolfgang Amadeus Mozart; he sang all three of them in German. Robeson believed that his singing helped him to lift the human spirit. He said, "I must feed the people with my songs."

Returning once more to England, Robeson began to prepare for the title role in Shakespeare's *Othello*, the first part that he had ever played in high school. He was to be only the second black man in a century to play Othello on the English stage. To improve his diction, he studied the speeches of ancient Roman orators, such as Cicero, and of English statesmen, such as Benjamin Disraeli. To uncover hidden meanings in Shakespeare's lines, he studied Old and Middle English, the languages spoken by the English in earlier centuries. He also learned Othello's lines in French, German, Russian, and Yiddish because he believed that each language presented Shakespeare's complex creation in a different light.

Robeson's intense preparation paid off. His performance as Othello was fluid and natural. On opening night, May 29, 1930, at the Savoy Theatre in London, he and his costars received 20 curtain calls. While Robeson continued to perform what would become one of his best-known roles, he also gave concert performances at the Savoy on Sundays. He dreamed of appearing in a production of *Othello* in the United States, but he knew that the play's subject matter including Othello's killing of his white wife would excite too much public controversy.

Robeson's acclaimed 1930 performance in Othello *was inspired by the parallels he felt between his own life and that of the character he played. Othello, he said, was "an alien among white people."*

Later in 1930, Robeson traveled to Berlin, Germany, to star in a production of *The Emperor Jones*. This gave him the chance to work with the innovative German stage director Max Reinhardt. Robeson then went to Switzerland to shoot the film *Borderline*, in which he played a stranger whose sudden appearance in a small village leads to tragedy. The movie was unusual in that it portrayed blacks in truly human situations. However, it was not popular with English audiences and was never shown in the United States. Eslanda appeared in the film as his wife.

In 1930, Robeson and Eslanda began to experience marital difficulties, and they agreed to separate for a while. Eslanda remained in England with three-year-old Pauli and began

Robeson's first major commercial film, The Emperor Jones, *enabled him to reach a wider audience than he could through a performance on the stage.*

to study African history and culture at the London School of Economics. During this time, she published a book on her husband entitled *Paul Robeson, Negro*. She wrote candidly about her husband's career and his extramarital love affairs, and she was also unsparing in her descriptions of racist attitudes in the United States.

Living apart from Eslanda, Robeson continued with his stage and singing career. In 1931, he appeared in a London production of Eugene O'Neill's drama *The Hairy Ape*. Later that year, audiences in New York got to hear him sing "Ol' Man River" for the first time when he appeared there on stage in *Show Boat*.

Shortly after Robeson returned to England in 1932, he and Eslanda managed to reconcile their differences. As always, he found the atmosphere in London to be stimulating to his growth as an artist. But he was not satisfied with having only the members of British high society for company. With the world in the grip of a massive economic depression, Robeson became keenly aware of the problems faced by millions of unemployed workers who were struggling to survive. He began to consider ways that he could bring attention to the plight of poor and oppressed people throughout the world.

Along with his growing commitment to the struggles of the working class, Robeson became more conscious of his racial heritage. Remembering how his father had talked about the great accomplishments of the kingdoms that had ruled Africa in earlier times, Robeson sought out African students who had come to England to further their education. At the time, most of Africa was divided into colonies ruled by Great Britain and other European nations. Among the students Robeson met in London were politically committed young men

Beginning in the mid-1920s, London became home to Robeson for more than a decade, although he often returned to America to work on various projects.

such as Kwame Nkrumah and Jomo Kenyatta, who would later lead African nationalist movements that would help win independence for their homelands. He also talked to black seamen and dockworkers, learning much about the conditions of blacks in other countries.

Robeson's budding interest in Africa led him to the study of African languages, and he was astonished by the flexibility and expressiveness of these ancient tongues. He spoke with newfound pride of his African heritage, and he engaged in frequent discussions about

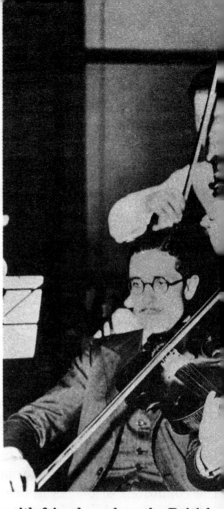

In the early 1930s, Robeson's musical repertoire began to include folk songs from all over the world.

cultural topics with friends such as the British novelist H. G. Wells and the Indian politician Jawaharlal Nehru. Gradually, Robeson began to see himself as a representative of all people of African descent. He wanted his music, plays, and films to convey the importance of

his identity as a living symbol for all black
people.

During previous concert tours, Robeson had
added a few songs by great European composers to his medley of black spirituals. Some
black writers in the United States had com-

mented that they were glad to see that he was moving beyond the limitations of black folk music. This attitude disturbed Robeson. He disapproved of the eagerness of many blacks, especially the young, to dismiss the spiritual wealth of their people's heritage in order to imitate whites and fit more comfortably into American society. Blues and spirituals were the true music of his people, Robeson believed, and blacks should treasure their precious folk idioms. Great European classical composers such as Igor Stravinsky were borrowing from black music, and jazz and other types of music developed by blacks were immensely popular throughout the world. Blacks must realize, Robeson said, that their music was inferior to none.

Although some blacks decided to become classical musicians and play Beethoven and Johannes Brahms, Robeson believed that this music was foreign to the black temperament. In 1933, he declared that in the future he would only sing music that he could understand and that he could feel in his soul. No longer would he sing works from an Italian or German opera if he could not find a connection between it and the black folk music he loved. However, he did not shut himself off from the music of other nations. He felt that he knew the "wail of the Hebrew," the "plaint of the Russian," and the emotions conveyed in other ethnic music.

As Robeson promoted black folk music to people all over the world, he developed an extremely close rapport with an international audience. His performances had a powerful effect on them, helping them to feel the pain, the fear, and the hope in his spirituals. Through his singing, he found a way to represent the true nature of the black race while at the same time making his music seem universal.

Robeson eventually added Mexican, Scottish, and Russian folk songs to his repertoire, singing them in their native language. The order of his songs in concert was eventually designed to show the development of folk music through the centuries and to highlight the interrelationships between the songs of different nations. He often continued to team with Lawrence Brown, who introduced him to many new kinds of music Brazilian and West Indian melodies, Flamenco music of Spain, works by contemporary Russian composers, the music of North and South American Indians, and songs from China, India, and many other Asian countries. While learning the songs of another nation, Robeson also studied the language. He was soon able to speak more than 20 languages.

While Robeson was concentrating on his singing career, his film career was given a boost in 1933 when he was asked to appear in the movie version of *The Emperor Jones*. A low-budget production shot in New York, the film gave him the chance to recreate the role he had made famous on the stage. The film was not a success, partly because it varied considerably from O'Neill's play. Black critics were incensed by the scenes that showed Robeson as a prisoner on a chain gang, as a participant in voodoo rituals, and as a deposed tyrant groveling in the dust. Robeson was unhappy that some of the most important dramatic devices that had been used in the play, such as the beating of drums to punctuate Brutus Jones's monologues, were either missing or were not used properly in the film. Nevertheless, his part in *The Emperor Jones* gave him the opportunity to play a strong, dignified black man. The film also increased his popularity with American audiences.

After returning to England in 1933, Robeson began to believe that his work had to be more closely tied in with his personal commitment to social justice. The emergence of German dictator Adolf Hitler's brutal Nazi regime was beginning to change the political climate in Europe. Both Germany and Italy were ruled by fascist dictatorships governments that exerted rigid control over their nations' political and economic systems.

Robeson had previously insisted that he was just an artist, that he did not understand politics. Now he started, he said, to "connect things up." He appeared in a production of *All God's Chillun Got Wings*, and the proceeds went to help Jewish refugees fleeing from persecution in Germany.

After becoming Robeson's musical partner in 1925, Lawrence Brown (shown here) continued to perform with the noted singer and actor for 40 years.

Inspired by his new political commitment, Robeson was excited by his next movie role: tribal chieftain Bosambo in the British film *Sanders of the River*. By the time he joined the production on location in Africa, thousands of feet of film had already been shot, showing authentic rituals of local tribes. Robeson believed that the film would give an honest depiction of African life and culture and would help to refute the popular belief that all Africans were ignorant savages.

When *Sanders of the River* was finally released, Robeson discovered to his horror that the film had been changed drastically. New scenes had been added, while others had been reedited, so that he scarcely recognized the film, which had been turned into a flag-waving apology for colonial imperialism. It showed three heroic white men fighting off a million bloodthirsty natives. Robeson's character had been twisted to look as though he were subservient to the British colonial rulers. The black press condemned him once more for playing a degrading role. This time he agreed.

Although Robeson was frustrated by his experiences with *Sanders of the River*, he was still interested in other film roles. At the end of 1934, he was invited to the Soviet Union by Russian film director Sergei Eisenstein, who wanted him to star in a movie about the Haitian leader Toussaint L'Ouverture. Ever since he had heard Claude McKay talk about his travels in the Soviet Union, Robeson had wanted to visit the country. He had even become fluent in the Russian language. The time was right, he decided, to satisfy his curiosity about the Soviet Union.

This concert bill from a performance by Robeson and Lawrence Brown reflects their strong interest in black spirituals.

"Let My People Go"

Chapter Five

"Let My People Go"

IN DECEMBER 1934, Robeson and his wife left London to visit the Soviet Union. Their travel plans included a journey by train through Germany. Robeson would have chosen a different route if he had realized how frightening the conditions were in Germany under Hitler's fascist regime. At the train station in Berlin, he and his wife were confronted by members of the feared Nazi guard unit known as the brownshirts. Robeson narrowly escaped being savagely beaten by the brownshirts, who hated Jews, gypsies, blacks, and other racial and ethnic groups that the Nazis

---

Robeson and his wife, Eslanda, return to the United States in 1935. His singing and acting career gave them the opportunity to travel all over the world.

considered to be inferior. The incident intensified Robeson's dislike for fascism and strengthened his commitment to the cause of freedom.

The people of the Soviet Union gave the Robesons a much different welcome. Recordings of Robeson's songs were extremely popular there, and the Russians greeted him as their great friend "Pavel Robesona." In Russia, Robeson discovered the freedom from racism that he had been seeking all his life. He believed in the Russian people and felt that they

Born into slavery in the mid-18th century, Toussaint L'Ouverture led a revolt that liberated Haiti from French rule in 1801.

were going to be the architects of a new world. Racial tolerance was taught in every school; the Soviet leaders were fostering cultural diversity among the country's different ethnic groups. To Robeson, the Soviet Union seemed to offer a greater equality to its citizens than did the United States.

For two weeks, Robeson stayed in Moscow as the guest of Sergei Eisenstein and met other black Americans. Many of them had become interested in going to the Soviet Union after hearing favorable accounts of life there through the American Communist party. Robeson joined other blacks in supporting the Soviets' calls for international brotherhood and their demands for the end of colonial rule in Africa and Asia.

Impressed by what he saw in Russia, Robeson decided to study the Marxist economic and political theories upon which the Soviets' communist state had been built. His love for the Soviet Union was based more on its racially liberated cultural climate than on its political doctrines. He ignored some of the less-than-pleasant facts about the country, including the mass purges of political opponents and the extermination of millions of uncooperative farmers that were carried out by Soviet dictator Joseph Stalin. What mattered most to Robeson was that the Soviets were committed to his own causes of workers' rights and racial equality.

After a pleasant stay in Moscow, the Robesons returned to London early in January 1935. Because of conflicts in their schedules,

Robeson was criticized for accepting a minor role in Show Boat, *which contained many black stereotypes. However, once the 1935 film was released, his performance was widely praised.*

Robeson and Eisenstein were never able to get together to make the film on Toussaint L'Ouverture. But Robeson was left with many fond memories of the Soviet Union and he intended to return there often.

Once again, Robeson became busy on the stage in England. He portrayed a dockhand who leads white and black workers in a fight to protect their labor union from mobsters who are trying to destroy it in the play *Stevedore*. He then traveled to the United States to give a concert tour and appear in a film production of *Show Boat*. It was his first big-budget Hollywood film, and he won generally outstanding reviews for his acting and singing. Some members of the black press criticized him for accepting a minor role, in which he played the shiftless loafer Joe. But most people believed that his rendition of "Ol' Man River" was worth the price of admission to the film.

By 1936, Robeson had decided that racial prejudice within the American film industry would make it unlikely that he could ever find the type of roles he wanted to play. He decided to center his film career in England instead. The next movie he made, *Song of Freedom,* was shot partly in Africa. In this movie, Robeson plays an English dockworker who not only becomes an operatic star but is discovered to have royal African ancestry. Robeson believed that *Song of Freedom* was the first film to portray blacks in a realistic fashion. However, it was never distributed in the United States and received little attention elsewhere.

Nevertheless, Robeson's film career soon began to soar. Later in 1936, he appeared as a dispossessed African ruler in a movie based on H. Rider Haggard's classic adventure story *King Solomon's Mines*. He was able to make changes in the film so that it would not become just another demonstration of British imperialist superiority. This film was preceded by his appearance on the stage in the title role of *Toussaint L'Ouverture*, a work by the Trinidadian playwright C. L. R. James.

Late in 1936, Robeson again traveled to the Soviet Union. He was accompanied by his nine-year-old son, Pauli, who had recently returned from a tour of Africa with Eslanda. Robeson stirred up some controversy after he enrolled Pauli in a Soviet school and told the American press that in the Soviet Union his son would be free of the racial prejudices that he would experience in any American school. Although Pauli later attended high school and college in the United States, Robeson was starting to be labeled by some Americans as an unpatriotic communist troublemaker.

Robeson appeared in two more British films

Robeson studied the African language Efik to prepare for his role as a dispossessed African king in the 1936 film King Solomon's Mines.

in 1937. *Jericho* (the version released in the United States was called *Dark Sands*) was an adventure film shot in Egypt. Robeson plays an American soldier who becomes the leader of a North African tribe. He then appeared in *Big Fella,* a film version of Claude McKay's novel *Banjo*. Robeson plays an honest, likable man who works on the docks in Marseilles, France. Eslanda Robeson and Paul Lawrence also had parts in this film. Both *Jericho* and *Big Fella* featured better images of blacks than most films usually did. However, they did not attract a large audience.

Robeson combined his cinematic work with efforts on behalf of groups that were fighting to turn back the growth of fascism in Europe. He gave benefit concerts to aid the struggle to free the formerly black-ruled African nation of Ethiopia, which had just been invaded and conquered by the armies of the Italian dictator Benito Mussolini's fascist regime. Fascism was then also on the march in Spain, where a civil war had broken out in 1936, pitting the German- and Italian-supported armies of General Francisco Franco's Nationalists against the republicans, who were battling to preserve democracy in Spain.

Along with battling fascism, Robeson became involved in the negritude movement, which had been begun by African students in

Paris to increase black consciousness and celebrate the achievements of blacks around the world. Maintaining his strong fascination with Africa, he wrote at the time, "I am a singer and an actor. I am primarily an artist. Had I been born in Africa, I would have belonged, I hope, to that family which sings and chants the glories and legends of the tribe."

Although Robeson was not African-born, he

Robeson was so impressed by the absence of racial prejudice in the Soviet Union that he enrolled his son, Paul, Jr., in a Soviet school.

believed that he could help his African brothers. In 1937, along with an old friend, the scholar and writer W. E. B. Du Bois, he founded the Council on African Affairs. An organization dedicated to assisting black African nationalist liberation movements, the council published a monthly newsletter, established an extensive research library on African studies, and held conferences and rallies to raise funds for liberation groups.

Robeson's love of freedom could not be confined to one continent. In December 1937, he joined a benefit concert for the Spanish republicans in which he sang "Ol' Man River," changing the song's famous line "I'm tired of livin', and feared of dyin'," to a cry of perseverance, "I must keep fightin', until I'm dyin'." The following year, he traveled to the battlefields in Spain and sang for the republican troops. While there, he met many members of the Abraham Lincoln Brigade, a unit composed of Americans who had volunteered to fight in the war against fascism. He took special pride in the number of black Americans who had joined the cause.

Returning to England, Robeson appeared in *Plant in the Sun*, a play about union organizing and sit-down strikes. He also became more involved in workers' causes, holding benefit concerts to support union activities. He had

Robeson on opening night of Jericho, with Princess Kouka, an African princess who costarred in the 1937 film.

Robeson often found the time in his busy singing and acting schedule to speak at rallies and conventions. His voice was powerfully effective in rousing support for the causes of freedom, equality, and workers' rights.

grown more aware of the tremendous gulf between the working class, which supported the republicans, and the British upper class, which largely ignored the Spanish civil war. Lending his voice to any cause that championed freedom and equality, he began to sever his connections with the upper class.

Proud Valley, the last film that Robeson made in England, was the one that satisfied him the most. In the film, he appears in the part of David Goliath, an American who befriends a community of Welsh coal miners and ultimately gives his life for them. Although he was again accused of playing the role of a black who is loyal to whites, the film championed him as a teacher, inspiring the coal miners to face their hardships with strength and dignity. *Proud Valley* also gave him the opportunity to sing his spirituals before the camera.

Robeson continued his travels in 1939. He and Paul Lawrence made an immensely popular concert tour of Scandinavia. While Adolf Hitler was proclaiming the inferiority of Jews, blacks, and other people whom he considered to be "subhuman," Robeson was being mobbed by his fans in Sweden, Norway, and Denmark. Aware of the power that great artists such as himself had over their audiences, Robeson said, "When I sing 'Let my people go,' I can feel sympathetic vibrations from my audience, whatever its nationality. It is no longer just a Negro song, it is a symbol of those seeking freedom from the dungeons of fascism in Europe today."

However, by the middle of 1939, he saw that there was little more he could do for the cause

of freedom in Europe. At the same time, the movement for racial equality in the United States had begun to gain some ground. Robeson believed that he should take part in this struggle. After living abroad for more than 11 years, he decided it was time to go home.

Members of the Abraham Lincoln Brigade, the volunteer force of Americans who fought against fascism in the Spanish civil war, return to the United States in 1938.

of freedom in Europe. At the same time, the
movement for racial equality in the United
States had begun to gain some ground. Robeson believed that he should take part in this
struggle. After living abroad for more than t...
years, he decided it was time to go home.

The
Voice of
the People

Chapter Six

The
Voice of
the People

WHEN THE 41-year-old Robeson returned to the United States in September 1939, he found that there seemed to be little change in race relations. Entering a fancy New York hotel to which he had been invited for a party, he was told to use the freight elevator because he was black. He no longer let such insults bother him; he simply told the hotel worker that freight elevators were for supplies and stepped inside the passenger elevator.

Robeson could see that some things in America had indeed changed for the better. The country was emerging from the deep

Seeking to improve race relations everywhere he went, Robeson voiced his concern for the welfare of people all around the world.

economic depression that had plagued it—and much of the rest of the world—during the 1930s. The New Deal policies of the administration of President Franklin D. Roosevelt were helping to restore economic prosperity and were putting millions of people back to work. Thousands of black workers were among those employed in giant government programs such as the Works Progress Administration (WPA) and the Civilian Conservation Corps. Roosevelt's wife, Eleanor, was widely respected for her humanitarian work and her efforts to improve racial understanding.

Robeson returned to the United States with the intention of using his voice to lead a crusade for the rights of blacks and all other downtrodden Americans. "It is my business," he said, "not only to tell the guy with the whip hand to go easy on my people but also to teach my people—all oppressed people—how to prevent that whip hand from being used against them."

Robeson began his crusade by giving a recital at the Mother African Methodist Episcopal (A.M.E.) Church in Harlem, where his brother Benjamin was a pastor. Robeson then joined the popular conductor Earl Robinson's American People's Chorus on the radio to sing a highly patriotic song, "Ballad for Americans." After Robeson and the chorus finished the long, moving song, the audience in the radio station's performance hall cheered for 20 minutes. They were applauding not only a spectacular performance but the words of a ballad whose sentiment closely matched Robeson's own beliefs:

> Are you an American?
> Am I an American?
> I'm just an Irish, Negro, Jewish, Italian,
> French, and English, Spanish, Russian,
> Chinese, Polish, Scotch, Hungarian,
> Litvak, Swedish, Finnish, Canadian,
> Greek and Turk, and Czech
> and double-Czech American.

Robeson's recording of "Ballad for Americans" established him as an extremely popular figure throughout the country. During 1940 and 1941, he gave numerous highly successful concerts. Early in 1941, he starred briefly in *John Henry*, a play about a heroic black miner. Later in the year, he and Eslanda bought a large house in Enfield, Connecticut. The United States was beginning to seem like home to them again.

After the Japanese bombed the American fleet at Pearl Harbor in Hawaii on December 7, 1941, Robeson saw his country enter World War II on the side of Great Britain and the Soviet Union against the German-Italian-Japanese alliance. He was glad to see his country join in the battle against Hitler's fascist forces, and he participated with other famous entertainers to help the war effort. He sang throughout the United States, speaking out on racial problems while his songs helped to buoy his countrymen's spirits as they struggled to win the war.

In 1942, Robeson returned to making movies. First, he narrated *Native Land,* a film about union organizing. Later in the year, he made *Tales of Manhattan,* which featured an all-star Hollywood cast: Charles Boyer, Rita Hayworth, Henry Fonda, Charles Laughton, Ginger Rogers, Edward G. Robinson, and Cesar Romero. Six different episodes in the movie track the fate of a dress coat as it passes from owner to owner—until the coat lands on a small plot of earth worked by a group of poor farmers, which includes Paul Robeson and Ethel Waters. The farmers find $43,000 in the coat, which they immediately share among themselves.

Robeson believed that he would be allowed to make changes in the picture while it was being made, but the inclusion of a racially offensive ending proved to him that he could not bend Hollywood to his will. Some critics who reviewed *Tales of Manhattan* saw in the finished film what must have attracted Robeson to the project in the first place: the film enabled Robeson to give a legitimate portrait of poverty, ignorance, and superstition. Some of his deepest convictions about labor and the common man are expressed in some of his lines. However, after making *Tales of Manhattan* Robeson was no longer interested in making movies in Hollywood.

Although films no longer appealed to Robeson, the theater still challenged him. In October 1943, he began appearing once more in *Othello*. The production was the event of the year on Broadway and never was Robeson so dominating a presence on the stage. After the play ran for 10 months in New York, the pro-

Robeson had the rare ability to move the entire public with a song. His voice, said one music critic, "is a voice in which deep bells ring."

Robeson with his wife, Eslanda, and their son, Paul, Jr., on the steps of their home in Enfield, Connecticut.

duction was taken on the road. While the war raged overseas, Robeson's performance as the tragic figure Othello helped to bind people of all races together. Maintaining his campaign

for racial equality, he refused to perform the play before segregated audiences.

While pursuing various artistic projects, Robeson labored heroically for an astonishing

Robeson's appearance in Tales of Manhattan *was his last attempt to come to terms with Hollywood. He said of the 1942 film, "It was the same old thing, the Negro solving his problem by singing his way to glory."*

W. E. B. Du Bois (right) congratulates Robeson on his speech at the 1949 World Peace Conference in Paris. Robeson had urged the conference to cultivate friendship between the United States and the Soviet Union.

number of causes: the Negro Playwrights Company, the Committee to Aid China, the Joint Anti-Fascist Refugee Committee, and of course the Council on African Affairs. In 1941, he spoke to the United Auto Workers in

Detroit and was made an honorary member of the National Maritime Union. He sang and spoke at a rally to free Earl Browder, the jailed leader of the American Communist party. After the U.S. entry into World War II at the end of 1941, he toured war plants and promoted war bonds. He waived his recital fee to sing for various causes: Russian War Relief, the Ford Workers Victory Chorus, the Labor Victory Rally at Yankee Stadium, and the Concert for Negro Soldiers. He spoke in Detroit, Michigan, for the black families of the Sojourner Truth Housing Project and called upon blacks to fight back against terrorist attacks by the Ku Klux Klan and other white racial supremacist groups. He spoke and sang at the North American Aircraft plant in Inglewood, California, at the invitation of the local United Auto Workers union and praised it for attempting to end discriminatory hiring practices.

Robeson received many awards for his efforts to help these causes. In 1943, he received the Abraham Lincoln Medal for notable and distinguished service in human relations. He also received the NAACP's Spingarn Medal, the most prestigious award given annually to a leading figure in the black community. In April 1945, he was selected by his fellow actors to read Carl Sandburg's funeral tribute to the late American president, Franklin Roosevelt. He also spoke and sang at the Negro Freedom Rally at New York's Madison Square Garden, was made an honorary member of the International Longshoremen's and Warehousemen's Union, and pleaded for an end to the practice of not hiring black players to participate in major league baseball.

Robeson's work as a prominent artist enabled him to become a leading spokesman against social injustice. In 1945, he sought equal employment opportunities for all Americans and called for an end to the poll tax, a fee paid by voters that was used to keep poor blacks from voting. He also performed as part of the first biracial United Service Organization's tour for troops in Germany, France, and Czechoslovakia, and he made a moving pilgrimage to the newly liberated Nazi concentration camps.

During this period, Robeson was as controversial as he was popular. He urged the U.S. government to share its nuclear secrets with the Soviet Union. He believed that such sharing was the best way to create international friendship and guarantee world peace.

Later in 1945, the United States, Great Britain, the Soviet Union, and their allies emerged victorious from World War II. Happy that the war against fascism had been won, Robeson looked forward to a time of great change in the years immediately ahead. He was hoping that great strides would be made toward achieving greater opportunities for blacks in the United States. Still active in his favorite role of Othello, he compared the Moor's world

The 1943 production of Othello, *which costarred Jose Ferrer (left) as Iago, was one of Robeson's crowning achievements as an actor. He was said to have given "unquestionably the finest portrayal of Shakespeare's tragic Moor. . . in this generation."*

with his own. He said that Othello's tragic end and "the complete destruction of all trusted and sacred values—all these suggest the shattering of a universe. . . . Now, interestingly enough, we stand at the end of one period in human history and before the entrance of a new. All our tenets and tried beliefs are challenged."

The colonial empires of Great Britain, France, and other European nations had been fatally weakened during World War II, and African countries were on the road to independence. Black Americans who had fought in the war against racial genocide and fascism in Europe were demanding an end to segregationist policies and racial violence in the United States. Although Robeson was committed to peace between nations, he was not hesitant in telling blacks to strike back against attackers. When asked if he believed in turning the other cheek, Robeson answered, "If someone hit me on one cheek, I'd tear his head off before he could hit me on the other one."

In the fall of 1946, Robeson stepped up his campaign for racial justice after a series of lynching incidents in which black servicemen were brutally murdered took place in the South. Robeson called on President Harry S. Truman to push for strict laws against lynching. Robeson also raised money to help relieve famine in South Africa and spoke out against that country's racist apartheid policies. He stood on picket lines with Canadian auto workers and fought for better labor conditions. He was elected to the Civil Rights Congress and strived to create a movement for racial equality.

But by 1947, relations between the Soviet Union and the United States had turned many people who had loved Robeson into supposed enemies. The Soviet Union was considered to be America's opponent, and left-wing groups in America were suspected of working for the Russians. The House Un-American Activities Committee was appointed by Congress to hunt for communists and other people who were sympathetic to the Soviet Union. Robeson was among those who were listed as being dangerous to the welfare of the United States.

In Peoria, Illinois, the Shriners organization canceled Robeson's contract to sing for them. In Albany, New York, the board of education tried to deny him the use of a junior high school for a concert. Max Yergan, a former co-worker on the Council on African Affairs, turned against Robeson, charging that the council was dominated by communists. The Transport Workers' Union withdrew Robeson's invitation to its annual dinner—the first of their dinners that he failed to attend in a decade. A biography of him for young people was banned from West Virginia's public libraries.

None of these denials deterred Robeson. After declining an invitation to run as the vice-presidential candidate for the newly formed Progressive party in 1948, he barnstormed the country in support of the liberal former secretary of agriculture Henry Wallace, who was bidding for the presidency. Robeson decided to support Wallace and the Progressives be-

Although Robeson turned down the Progressive party nomination for vice-president in 1948, he traveled around the country speaking in support of Henry Wallace, the party's presidential candidate.

Violence broke out at Robeson's concert appearances at Peekskill, New York, in 1949. Some concertgoers who supported Robeson were attacked by rock-throwing mobs; other fans were dragged from their cars and beaten.

cause he thought that Truman and the Democrats were not fighting hard enough for voting rights, anti-lynching, and fair-employment-opportunity legislation in Congress. He opposed a new law for the registration of Com-

munist party members and of members of
organizations that allegedly were connected
to the communists. He viewed the law as a
violation of the rights of American citizens.

In April 1949, Robeson joined other supporters of world peace at Paris for the World Peace Congress. At this conference, he made a statement that it was unthinkable for black Americans to fight in a war against the Soviet Union in the service of a nation that had enslaved them for so many generations. His remarks created an uproar in the United States. Many black leaders spoke out against him and assured the public that blacks would be willing to defend their country against the Soviets, if necessary.

Robeson's return to the United States after the Paris peace congress was marked by violence. People coming to his concert in Peekskill, New York, on August 27, 1949, were greeted by a rock-throwing mob shouting, "Go back to Russia, you niggers!" Although a group of volunteers was able to protect the concert grounds for a short while, the mob broke through and went on a rampage, destroying the stage, overturning cars, and beating the concertgoers.

Refusing to be intimidated, Robeson held another concert in Peekskill eight days later. This time, more police were on hand to maintain order, and volunteers formed a protective line for the crowd that had come to hear Robeson, the musician Pete Seeger, and others sing and speak out for equality, freedom, and peace. However, after the performance, a

owling mob led by the American Legion
hrew rocks through the windows of vehicles
riven by concertgoers. People were dragged
rom their cars and beaten. The police stood
y and did nothing while more than 140 of the
eople attending the concert were injured.

Jackie Robinson, who in 1947 had become
he first black man to play baseball in the ma-
or leagues, had previously said that Robeson's
'aris statements sounded "very silly." How-
ver, after the Peekskill riots, Robinson joined
vith other black spokesmen in protesting
gainst the climate of racial intolerance in
America. Robeson bravely continued a concert
our sponsored by the Council on African Af-
airs despite the danger posed by picketing
American Legionnaires and the Veterans of
'oreign Wars. Speaking before an audience in
Harlem, he said, "I am born and bred in this
America of ours. I want to love it. I love part
f it. But it's up to the rest of America when
shall love it with the same intensity that I
ove the Negro people from whom I sprang."

In the charged atmosphere of the nuclear
ge, the racial equality that Robeson de-
nanded was considered to be a far less press-
ng matter by government officials than na-
ional defense. As shown by the Peekskill riots,
nany Americans were willing to use extreme
iolence against people who questioned their

One of the many ways in which Robeson (second from left) lobbied against racism and discrimination in America was by refusing to perform for segregated audiences.

nation's commitment to peace and justice. And many Americans, both black and white, had been convinced by Robeson's enemies that he was disloyal to his country. Robeson did not believe his friendship for the people of the Soviet Union threatened the United States in

any way, but his views were becoming increasingly unpopular.

In 1949, the Soviet Union named one of its highest peaks in Robeson's honor. When word of this reached the United States, the damage to Robeson's reputation was complete.

many evil things were beginning to break down in reputation.

In 1949, the Soviet Union named one of its highest peaks in Robeson's honor. When word of this reached the United States, the damage to Robeson's reputation was complete.

Exiled
in America

Chapter Seven

Exiled
in America

ROBESON'S UNPOPULARITY increased in 1950. He was not allowed to appear on television with Eleanor Roosevelt, his portrait was banned in Boston, and—after he protested American intervention in the war between North and South Korea—his passport was withdrawn. He filed a suit almost immediately against Secretary of State Dean Acheson in order to regain his right to travel abroad. Then he launched a newspaper called *Freedom* so he could voice his views.

Most Americans thought that Robeson was

Robeson helps to celebrate the 33rd anniversary of the Russian Revolution at the Soviet Embassy in Washington, D.C., under the watchful eyes of dictator Joseph Stalin. Robeson's support of the Soviet Union was largely based on the lack of racism he found in the Russian people—not on Stalin's political beliefs.

Robeson and his lawyer, James T. Wright (left), battled the State Department for eight years in an effort to regain Robeson's right to travel abroad after his passport was revoked in 1950.

prevented from traveling because he was a communist. After all, he refused to deny being a communist. Wasn't that enough proof?

Robeson argued that the government was not so concerned with him. It was more concerned with the 14 million blacks in America, the 40 million in the Caribbean and Latin

America, and the 150 million in Africa who looked to him as a spokesman. If he continued to stir up blacks with his talk of freedom and peace, the result might be worldwide revolution.

Freedom and travel have been strongly linked in America ever since the days of slavery, when slaves were not allowed to travel freely. In an attempt to clarify his position, Robeson quoted the former slave turned antislavery leader Frederick Douglass: "I deny the charge that I am saying a word against the institutions of America, or the people as such. What I have to say is against slavery and the slaveholders."

Robeson took part in many court battles to regain his passport. He was told to stop making speeches, and he was sometimes threatened with violence. But he continued to speak out against colonialism in Africa. He denounced the Korean War, insisting that the United States was supporting a dictatorial government. He believed that this action in Asia was a first step toward greater U.S. involvement overseas and would eventually result in wars that would decimate the populations of Asia, Africa, and other areas. He insisted that black Americans should have no part in such policies, but should stay home and fight for freedom in Georgia, Mississippi, Alabama, Texas, and the ghettos of Chicago and New York.

As a result of his outspokenness, Robeson was boycotted throughout America even though he was not charged with any illegal activities and was never arrested or put on trial. W. E. B. Du Bois, who, like Robeson, had had his passport stripped from him by the State Department because of his supposedly subversive statements, declared Robeson the best-known American on earth, a man whose voice was familiar on every continent. Only America denied him honor and rights.

In places such as Peekskill, Robeson was hated; but in Harlem, where he made his home, he was loved. He regularly attended Mother A.M.E. Zion Church, where his brother Benjamin continued to preach. In the Harlem church, he was warmly reminded of earlier days with his father's congregations in Princeton, Westfield, and Somerville.

Each time a court denied Robeson his passport, his words and actions grew more inflammatory. With the German novelist-in-exile Thomas Mann, he sponsored the "American Peace Crusade" and its "Peace Pilgrimage" to Washington. Heading the New York delegation of the Civil Rights Congress, he presented a petition to the United Nations protesting the U.S. government's policies toward blacks. The petition declared the United States guilty of racial genocide for subjecting millions of black Americans to conditions that led inevitably to poverty, disease, and premature death. Robeson continued to tell his people that they should not look upon the Soviet Union as their enemy and that they should refuse to partici-

Prohibited from crossing the Canadian border for a scheduled concert in 1952, Robeson performed at Peace Arch Park, on the border between the state of Washington and British Columbia.

pate in wars that he claimed only furthered
U.S. imperialism at the expense of oppressed
native populations.

The more Robeson was persecuted by the
government and right-wing organizations, the
more radical his political stance became. Im-
patient with the gradual improvement promised to his people, he announced that "the time
is now." He rejected calls for black separatism,
but he was equally opposed to assimilation. He
demanded political, cultural, and economic independence for black Americans.

Before the civil rights movement had gained
much strength and a decade before "Black
Power" became a popular slogan, Robeson
called for "Negro power." Confronted with in-
creasing racial violence, he insisted that blacks
had not only the right but the duty to defend
themselves, their communities, and their prop-
erty. He spoke forcefully against the racism
directed at American Indians, Mexican-Ameri-
cans, Puerto Ricans, and Asian-Americans.

Accepting an invitation in 1952 to speak to
a meeting of the Mine, Mill and Smelter Workers' Union of Vancouver, British Columbia,
Robeson attempted to cross the Canadian border, but State Department officials warned
him that if he left the United States, he would
be subject to five years' imprisonment and a
$10,000 fine. So Robeson spoke and sang to

the union members over the telephone from Seattle, Washington. The union then arranged for a concert at Peace Arch Park, on the border between the state of Washington and the province of British Columbia. More than 40,000 supporters came to hear him and to cheer him.

Soon after the concert, Robeson became the vice-chairman of the newly created Peace Liaison Committee for Asian and Pacific Peace. He protested the jailing of his old friend Jomo

U.S. involvement in the Korean War cost the lives of 34,000 Americans in battle. Robeson believed that his country had no right to intervene in the war between North and South Korea.

Kenyatta and other Kenyan freedom fighters who were trying to win their country's independence from Great Britain. The National Church of Nigeria named Robeson a "Champion of African Freedom" for his "selfless service to Africa." The All-India Peace Council circulated a plea for the return of his passport. The Soviet Union awarded him its highest honor, the Stalin Peace Prize.

More and more, Robeson was convinced that the United States was using the cold war as

a tool to oppress the world's non-white populations. As early as 1954, he protested U.S. involvement in Vietnam on the same grounds
that he opposed intervention in Korea. In a little over a decade, participation in the Viet-
namese civil war would become the most un-

Acting in his capacity as chairman of the Council on African Affairs, Robeson (second from left) meets with African political leaders. The council fought for African independence and Afro-American pride until it was disbanded in 1955 under pressure from the U.S. government.

popular military action in U.S. history. But in 1954 Robeson's was a lonely if indomitable voice of resistance.

Black leaders increasingly disassociated themselves from Robeson. Photographs showing him meeting with a leader of the NAACP were removed from the organization's files and destroyed. Even though upper-class blacks seemed to be displeased with him for expressing his views so vocally, Robeson continued to take seriously the obligation to his people that was first expressed by his father.

At the age of 56, Robeson no longer earned as much money as he once did. His annual income, as high as $100,000 in 1947, sank to $6,000. Ingenious arrangements were often required for him to get work. In 1954, he was asked to sing on the soundtrack of Dutch filmmaker Joris Ivens's *Song of the Rivers*. Banned from all American recording studios, he was forced to use an improvised studio in a quiet corner of Benjamin Robeson's parsonage. The studio was constructed by his son, who had become an electrical engineer. The recording required many takes to compensate for noises coming from the street outside the church.

When the film was released, Robeson was surprised to discover how many famous artists had worked on the film. The score was by Russian composer Dimitri Shostakovich. The original German lyrics were by playwright Bertolt Brecht. The film's commentary was by French novelist Vladimir Pozner. And advertising for the film featured a poster created by Pablo Picasso.

Robeson's concerts at Peace Arch Park,

which began in 1952, continued until 1955, when the State Department decided to allow Robeson to travel to Canada. But this triumph was followed by other setbacks. The Council on African Affairs was disbanded and *Freedom* suspended publication. Robeson stated that harassment by the FBI and other government organizations had forced the council and the newspaper to suspend operations. In addition, the State Department continued to refuse to return his passport until he signed an oath stating that he was not a communist.

In 1956, the House Un-American Activities Committee finally summoned Robeson to appear at a hearing to determine whether or not he was a communist. That same year, his name was removed from the listings of the 1917 and 1918 All-American football teams.

International protests against the U.S. government's restrictions on Robeson became more pronounced. Members of the British Actors' Equity Association voted to use their influence to bring him to Britain so he could perform there. At around the same time, 5,000 miners in Wales gathered to hear him sing for them over the phone. Indian Prime Minister Indira Gandhi organized a "Paul Robeson Day" in her country.

In 1958, after Robeson's 60th birthday was celebrated in West Germany, East Germany,

Jackie Robinson, the first black major-league baseball player, testifies before the House Un-American Activities Committee about political statements made by Robeson. Robinson later sided with Robeson in his right to assert his beliefs.

the Soviet Union, China, and many African nations, a small press in Harlem published a book he had written, *Here I Stand*. Although the book contained a brief autobiographical chapter, it primarily expressed the beliefs that had motivated Robeson's public and private actions for more than 30 years, including his "The time is now" theme and his call for all black Americans to support the civil rights movement. The book was dedicated to the future of the courageous black children who in 1957 had helped to end segregation in the public school system in Little Rock, Arkansas.

The silence with which the American press greeted *Here I Stand* was astounding. Not one major newspaper or magazine in America mentioned the book when it was first published. Not only was the book not reviewed; it was not even included on lists of books being published. However, *Here I Stand* received tremendous international coverage after appearing simultaneously in several foreign-language editions.

Most of America's black press embraced the beliefs that Robeson expressed in *Here I Stand*. Although he had previously received abuse from some of the black community, the tone of the book was conciliatory toward these groups.

W. E. B. Du Bois called the government's

A smiling Robeson celebrates his 60th birthday in 1958, after more than a decade of persecution. "The artist must elect to fight for freedom or slavery," he maintained. "I have made my choice. I had no alternative."

persecution of Paul Robeson one of the most contemptible actions in modern history. Du Bois's sentiment began to be shared by many black Americans who had previously listened to the attacks on Robeson by moderate black leaders such as Walter White of the NAACP. In no small part due to the growing civil rights movement, Paul Robeson began to be perceived as a forerunner of black rights. In *Here I Stand*, he urged his people to stand up and be counted in the crusade for racial justice: "We have the power of numbers, the power of organization and the power of spirit. . . . Mass action—in political life and elsewhere—is Negro power in motion: and it is the way to win."

Here I Stand also contained a thorough description of Robeson's continuing battle to regain his passport. However, before the book was published, the Supreme Court ruled that the withholding of his passport was illegal, as Robeson had maintained it was. The ruling enabled Robeson to begin traveling once again, thus ending a period of eight years during which he had been forced to remain in America against his will.

Free
At Last

Chapter Eight

Free at Last

ROBESON ANNOUNCED his passport victory at the end of a sold-out show at Carnegie Hall in May 1958, his first concert appearance in New York in 10 years. Within two months of this announcement, he began a concert tour of Europe. The tour started in London, where he signed contracts for a television series covering his concerts. One month later, he sang on Moscow television. A week after that, he visited Soviet premier Nikita Khrushchev.

The 60-year-old Robeson's European tour ended triumphantly, with him singing the

Robeson returns to the United States in 1963. The press attributed his leaving the Soviet Union to a disillusionment with communism. However, he had come home simply to retire.

Robeson is greeted by his "beloved Soviet peoples" as he arrives in the Soviet Union for a concert tour in 1958.

spiritual "Jacob's Ladder" at St. Paul's Cathedral in London. This performance enabled him to become the first black to stand at the lectern. More than 4,000 people listened inside the cathedral, while another 5,000 stood outside.

Touched by this reception, Robeson considered making his home in London once again. But the years of struggle had ruined his health, a fact that was made evident during his second European tour in late 1958. Shortly after celebrating New Year's Eve as

Khrushchev's guest at a Kremlin ball, Robeson fell ill and was hospitalized in Moscow.

As his physical condition became steadily weaker, Robeson realized that he would not be able to perform in public for much longer. Yet there was still one performance that he wanted to give. More than anything, he wanted to play *Othello* at Stratford-on-Avon, Shakespeare's birthplace in England. Doctors gave him permission to perform the play in April 1959, and it marked his last stage performance.

By 1960, Robeson was back in Moscow,

Freedom Riders sit in the "whites only" waiting room of the Montgomery, Alabama, bus terminal in 1961. Riding buses through the South to test the racial climate, this interracial group of civil rights activists was frequently met by violent mobs.

singing and speaking to plant workers. With Khrushchev, he attended a special production marking the 100th anniversary of playwright Anton Chekhov's birth. He then toured Wales and traveled to East Germany. In November, he began a concert tour of Australia and New Zealand. This was his last concert tour because his great voice had started to weaken.

During another trip to the Soviet Union in April 1961, Robeson had to seek treatment in a Moscow hospital for physical exhaustion. He spent the next two years in and out of hospitals and nursing homes in England and East Germany. He began to suffer increasingly from

dizzy spells caused by circulatory problems.

In December 1963, Robeson and his wife, Eslanda, returned to Harlem. It was reported in the newspapers that he was disappointed with the communism of the Soviet Union and East Germany. But as with so much the press had said of him, the statement was untrue. Plagued with a circulatory illness, he was simply coming home to retire.

Despite his illness, Robeson continued to issue periodic messages. In August 1964, he once again stated his support of the civil rights movement and mourned for the victims of racially motivated murders that had recently occurred in Alabama and Mississippi. He did not think the time had yet come to sing the words from an old Negro spiritual, "Thank God Almighty, we're free at last," but he was glad that at last blacks were being stirred into action.

In 1965, a special salute to Paul Robeson was staged at the Hotel Americana in New York. The ceremony was led by actor Ossie Davis

Dr. Martin Luther King, Jr., leads a civil rights march from Selma, Alabama, to Montgomery, Alabama, in 1965. Marches such as this one helped the civil rights movement to gain national attention.

and actress Ruby Dee, with novelist James Baldwin a featured speaker. Despite this celebration, 1965 was one of the saddest years in Robeson's life, for it was the year in which Eslanda died. They had been married for more than 40 years, and though it had been an emotionally demanding relationship, it had clearly been an enduring one. Eslanda had shared in his work and his political activities and had loyally supported him during the years that he was blacklisted. She had often been as outspoken for human rights as he had been.

After Eslanda died, a frail and sickly Robeson moved to Philadelphia, Pennsylvania, to live with his sister, Marion. His addresses to his fans and supporters continued, but he rarely appeared in public. Instead, he watched on television as other people made the kinds of statements for which he had been persecuted. He was pleased to see that America had become more receptive to freedom of expression. He wrote, "Today it is the Negro artist who does *not* speak out who is considered to be out of line."

New honors came Robeson's way in the 1970s. In 1971, a students' center at Rutgers University was named in his honor. *Ebony* magazine proclaimed him one of the 10 most important black men in American history. National Educational Television, the forerunner

of the Public Broadcasting System, telecast
an Emmy Award-winning series on his life.
When a ceremony in honor of his 75th birthday was held at Carnegie Hall in 1973, he sent
a special message to the celebrants, saying he
was still the same man who had dedicated so
much of his life to the worldwide cause of
freedom, peace, and brotherhood.

Here I Stand, the book Robeson had published in 1958, was finally reviewed by major
newspapers. In 1974, he was honored by the
American Actors' Equity Association and the
AFL-CIO with the establishment of an award
in his name. Perhaps the sweetest award for
Robeson was an honorary Doctor of Law degree given to him by Lincoln University, his
father's alma mater.

On December 12, 1975, Robeson was admitted to Presbyterian University Hospital in
Philadelphia after suffering a minor stroke.
He died on January 23, 1976, at the age of 77.
More than 5,000 mourners attended the me-
morial service at Mother A.M.E. Zion Church
in Harlem.

A proud man with a profound understanding
of other people's hopes and desires, Robeson
attacked a variety of social issues at the risk
of his own career. Deeply loved—and at times
deeply hated—he never bowed to the weighty
pressures placed upon him as he fought over

Robeson used the prestige and influence he gained from his artistic career to focus attention not only on the plight of black Americans but on the troubles of persecuted people everywhere.

these issues, and his lifelong efforts to promote civil rights eventually silenced insults that were often hurled at him. Today, there is little disagreement that Paul Robeson was more than just a powerful singer and a talented actor. He was also a man of firm beliefs and enormous integrity.

CHRONOLOGY

1898	Born Paul Leroy Robeson in Princeton, NJ
1904	Robeson's mother, Maria, dies
1915	Robeson enrolls at Rutgers University
1917	First of two selections to the All-American football team
1918	Elected to Phi Beta Kappa honors society
1919	Moves to New York City; enrolls at Columbia Law School
1920	Makes acting debut in *Simon the Cyrenian*
1921	Marries Eslanda Goode
1922	Plays in National Football League championship game for the Akron Indians
1923	Joins New York law firm
1924	Appears in *The Emperor Jones* and *All God's Chillun Got Wings*
1925	Makes concert debut with Lawrence Brown
1927	Birth of son, Pauli
1928	Moves to London, England; appears in *Show Boat*
1929	First performance at Carnegie Hall in New York
1930	Appears in *Othello*
1934	Visits the Soviet Uniion
1935	Appears in film version of *Show Boat*
1939	Appears in *Proud Valley*; resettles in the United States
1943	Awarded Abraham Lincoln Medal
1945	Awarded Spingarn Medal; joins USO tour
1948	Attends World Peace Congress in Paris, France; concert at Peekskill, NY, results in riot
1950	Passport is revoked; establishes *Freedom* newspaper
1952	Awarded Stalin Peace Prize
1956	Testifies before HUAC
1958	*Here I Stand* is published; passport is reinstated
1959	Final performance of *Othello*
1965	Wife, Eslanda, dies
1976	Robeson dies in Philadelphia, PA

FURTHER READING

Brown, Lloyd L. *Lift Every Voice for Paul Robeson.* New York: Freedom Associates, 1951.

Foner, Philip S. *Paul Robeson Speaks.* Secaucus, NJ: Citadel Press, 1978.

Gilliam, Dorothy Butler. *Paul Robeson: All-American.* Washington, DC: New Republic Book Company, 1976.

Graham, Shirley. *Paul Robeson, Citizen of the World.* New York: Julian Messner, Inc., 1946.

Hamilton, Virginia. *Paul Robeson: The Life and Times of a Free Black Man.* New York: Harper & Row, 1974.

Hoyt, Edwin P. *Paul Robeson: The American Othello.* New York: World Publishing, 1967.

Nazel, Joseph. *Paul Robeson, Biography of a Proud Man.* Los Angeles: Holloway House Publishing Company, 1980.

Robeson, Eslanda Goode. *Paul Robeson, Negro.* London: Gollancz, 1930.

Robeson, Paul. *Here I Stand.* Boston: Beacon Press, 1971.

Robeson, Susan. *The Whole World in His Hands.* Secaucus, NJ: Citadel Press, 1981.

INDEX

PICTURE CREDITS

SCOTT EHRLICH was born in White Plains, New York. Among his many projects, he has written about a number of his favorite subjects, ranging from art and athletics to drama and dinosaurs. He currently lives in Randolph, New Jersey.

NATHAN IRVIN HUGGINS is W.E.B. Du Bois Professor of History and Director of the W.E.B. Du Bois Institute for Afro-American Research at Harvard University. He previously taught at Columbia University. Professor Huggins is the author of numerous books, including *Black Odyssey: The Afro-American Ordeal in Slavery, The Harlem Renaissance,* and *Slave and Citizen: The Life of Frederick Douglass.*